Original title:
Botanic Ballads

Copyright © 2025 Creative Arts Management OÜ
All rights reserved.

Author: Christian Leclair
ISBN HARDBACK: 978-1-80567-069-8
ISBN PAPERBACK: 978-1-80567-149-7

Melodies from the Meadow's Heart

In the meadow green, a bonny sight,
Daisy dances with all her might.
A dandelion puff takes to the sky,
Singing on breeze, oh me, oh my!

Grasshoppers chirp in a jazzy beat,
While ladybugs waltz on tiny feet.
A squirrel in shades, strikes a pose,
Twirling round, oh, how he glows!

With petals bright, and stems so tall,
The tulips giggle at the butterfly's call.
"Keep it down!" shouts an old wise tree,
"Your frolics are fun, but let's drink some tea!"

As the sun dips low, the night takes flight,
Fireflies disco, glowing in the night.
Every bloom joins in this merry spree,
Swaying away, in sweet harmony!

Harvesting the Heartbeats

In the garden, weeds do dance,
Tomatoes prance in summer's chance.
Carrots giggle as they grow,
While beans play tag, a lively show.

The sun laughs loud, the rain will wink,
Eggplants wobble, they tease and think.
Radishes in capes, they dash about,
'Tis a frolic that leaves no doubt!

Melodies of the Meadow

Crickets chirp a silly tune,
Butterflies leap, they'll swoon by noon.
Daisies wear hats, quite extravagance,
As bumblebees buzz, they take a chance.

The brook hums soft, a giggly flow,
While frogs declare a dance-off show.
Grasshoppers jump, a comic spree,
Nature's jesters, wild and free!

The Language of Lilies

Lilies gossip beneath the moon,
Their fragrant whispers make hearts swoon.
Dandelions puff with glee,
Blowing wishes, wild and free.

The tulips trade in playful puns,
While violets hide from startled runs.
In vibrant hues, they share their jokes,
A floral laugh that always awoke!

Rhythms of the Rooted Realm

In the soil, secrets murmur low,
Worms twist and turn, a squiggly show.
Oak trees dance with a creaky beat,
While the shadows caper at their feet.

The roots write rhymes in the dark,
Underneath where adventures hark.
Fungi giggle in their little caps,
Mushroom parties with all the chaps!

The Requiem of the Rosewood

In the garden, whispers play,
The rosewood laughs at woes of day.
With branches bent, it tells a tale,
Of squirrels who dance, and leaves that sail.

A woodpecker's tap, a comical beat,
While rabbits hop, oh what a feat!
They hold a feast on leafy treats,
And gossip flows as nature greets.

Sketches Amongst the Shrubs

Among the shrubs, a secret crew,
The hedgehogs plan their night debut.
They don top hats, so dapper and prim,
While the daisies giggle, their petals brim.

With every rustle, a joke is spun,
The garden's laughter—it's so much fun!
A bumblebee buzzes a tune so sweet,
As worms throw shade from underground seats.

The Serenade of Summer's Return

Summer's back with a sunny grin,
The daisies dance, let the fun begin!
With each warm breeze, they sway and twirl,
As butterflies gossip in a colorful whirl.

The ants march proud in their tiny parade,
While ladybugs play, unafraid.
A sunburned cactus waves hello,
As lizards laugh at the sun's warm glow.

Sonnet of the Seasons

Spring brings laughter on budding trees,
While winter chuckles, 'Catch me if you please!'
In autumn's arms, a pumpkin's grin,
And summer's songs play, inviting in.

Each season's tale, a playful jest,
With nature's humor, we're truly blessed.
From frosty nights to sunlit days,
The garden's giggles—oh how it sways!

Hymn of the Hollowed Trees

In the woods where shadows play,
The trees giggle in their own way.
With branches bending, oh so bold,
They whisper secrets, tales retold.

A squirrel dances, tail a-twirl,
While acorns down like marbles whirl.
The owls hoot in a comical tone,
As nighttime creeps, their laughter's grown.

Mossy cushions, nature's seat,
Where chipmunks gather for a treat.
They munch on nuts with tiny hands,
While joking about all life's demands.

Lively leaves in breezes swirl,
As trees hold court in nature's whirl.
With every creak and crack they prance,
To frolic in this leafy dance.

Rhythms of the Rooted Realm

Roots like dancers twist below,
In tangled grooves, they steal the show.
Giggling grasshoppers jump and sway,
While earthworms wiggle, 'Come what may!'

Sunlight streams, a warm embrace,
On blossoms' faces, smiles replace.
Bees buzz around in silly haze,
As flowers nod in sunny praise.

Underneath a leafy dome,
Fungi sprout, making their home.
A mushroom cap in a funny hat,
Grows near a hedgehog, oh so fat!

With roots that tickle and tease the ground,
Nature's laughter can be found.
The forest floor, a stage of glee,
Where all join in harmony.

Petals in the Breeze

Petals dance like butterflies,
In the wind, their laughter flies.
Tulips giggle, daisies wink,
While dandelions blow and think.

They whisper jokes in colors bright,
As bees come buzzing to delight.
A ladybug, on a roll,
Claims a petal for its stroll.

The roses tease with fragrance sweet,
While sunflowers sway, a rhythmic beat.
With every breeze, a ticklish thrill,
The garden's joy, it cannot spill.

In every hue and nature's cheer,
Laughter lingers, always near.
So join the flowers, take a seat,
In joy-filled blooms, life is sweet.

Serenade of the Sunlit Meadow

In sunlit fields where ponies prance,
Wildflowers join in a merry dance.
Bouncing bunnies hop with glee,
While butterflies sip on nectar tea.

The grass all giggles beneath the feet,
As kids run wild with boundless heat.
They play and roll in joyful spree,
With nature's games, so wild and free.

A gopher peeks out, all in jest,
Wearing a cap, he joins the fest.
With daisies tucked behind his ear,
He shares a laugh, spreading the cheer.

The sun sets low, their shadows grow,
As crickets croak their evening show.
In every heart, the meadow's song,
A timeless ballad, bright and strong.

Whispers of the Wildwood

In the wildwood's deep embrace,
A squirrel wore a pair of lace.
It twirled and laughed, what a sight!
Even the trees joined in at night.

A rabbit threw a grand old bash,
With carrots served in a wild flash.
They danced 'neath the full moon's glow,
Even the owls put on a show!

Witty foxes cracked some jokes,
While hedgehogs played the merry folks.
With giggles spreading branch to branch,
The wildwood sang, a funny ranch!

As dawn approached, the fun must end,
But laughter's roots will always tend.
In whispers soft, they took their leave,
The wildwood dreams we still believe.

Chronicles of the Chrysalis

A chubby caterpillar named Clyde,
Declared he'd take a wiggly ride.
He climbed a leaf and tried to soar,
But landed in a garden store.

With discounts on cocoons galore,
He tried on stripes, then left the floor.
A butterfly named Bella teased,
"Your fashion sense is rather squeezed!"

So Clyde, with style now in tow,
Came out to join the garden show.
In vibrant hues, he flaunted flair,
Leaving all the daisies in despair.

He twirled around with great delight,
While saying, "Chrysalis? It's a fright!
Embrace the change, break out with glee,
Who knew a worm could dance so free?

The Verse of Verdant Valleys

In valleys green, the flowers spoke,
Their petals twirling, a playful joke.
A daisy claimed, "I'm royalty!"
While others vowed, "We'll set you free!"

The sunbeam giggled, giving chase,
As dandelions formed a race.
They puffed and blew, "Who'll fly the best?"
But ended up a fluffy mess.

A little bean, with dreams so tall,
Dreamed he would one day be a wall.
But tripped on roots, fell flat and said,
"I think I'm better off instead!"

Yet in the vale where laughter grows,
The plants unite to strike a pose.
In leafy hats and tangled vines,
They tell their tales with silly lines.

The Chronicle of the Colorful Canopy

High above, the branches sway,
Where birds exchange the silliest play.
A parrot painted in bright hues,
Told tales of shoes that danced like blues.

"Have you seen a tree that sings?"
Asked a branch, sprouting quirky wings.
"Last night it crooned a love-struck song,
Though the notes were really quite wrong!"

The wise old owl, with spectacles on,
Declared, "In trees, we all belong.
So shake a leaf or two tonight,
Let's 'branch' out for some fun and fright!"

The canopy burst with laughter bright,
With giggly squirrels taking flight.
Through colors wild, the fun grew grand,
In the chronicles of fun, they stand!

Poems from the Pollen Pathways

In the garden, bees collide,
Wearing hats of pollen pride.
They dance on blooms with glee,
A buzzing circus, oh so free!

Petunias giggle in the breeze,
With secrets whispered to the trees.
Laughter echoes, flowers sway,
In this wild and fragrant play!

Daisies wear their sunbeam crowns,
While clovers tell their joke-laden frowns.
The tulips shout, 'We are so bright!
No need for gloom on this fine night!'

In the moonlight, beetles dance,
Cartwheeling through their leafy expanse.
With every poke and playful glide,
Nature chuckles, side by side.

Narratives of Nature's Palette

The daisies tell of sunlit days,
While violets blush in purple haze.
Each petal boasts a funny tale,
Of raindrops' trips and wind's exhale.

The marigolds wear coats of gold,
While sunflowers shout, 'Behold! Behold!'
Their faces turn with comic flair,
As clouds play peek-a-boo in air.

Ferns whisper jokes in shady nooks,
While butterflies share their picture books.
With every flutter, laughter flows,
In this story where no one knows!

But the lilacs smile with scents so sweet,
Inviting all to dance on their feet.
A garden party, bold and bright,
Where nature laughs throughout the night.

The Memory of Mossy Stones

In quiet glades where shadows creep,
Mossy stones hold secrets deep.
They chuckle softly, wise and old,
Sharing stories of courage bold.

With rumbles of laughter, roots entwine,
As flowers tease, 'We're quite divine!'
The stones reply, 'We're quite aware,
You bloom so bright without a care.'

The ants parade in frantic line,
Claiming all the crumbs as mine!
While mushrooms giggle, round and stout,
As woodland whispers dance about.

When sunlight warms the forest floor,
The stones break out in laughter's roar.
For every drop of dew that gleams,
A memory of nature's dreams.

Adoration of the Alpine Blooms

On mountain tops, the flowers grin,
As winds surround them in a spin.
They laugh at clouds so low and gray,
Saying, 'We'll shine, come what may!'

With alpine tunes and breezy notes,
The blossoms trap the chirping goats.
They joke and jive in frosty air,
Daring the snowflakes to declare.

The edelweiss wear frosty hats,
While poppies tease the nearby rats.
'Just look at us, we're fierce and bold,
In winter's grasp, we shun the cold!'

At twilight's hour, they start their song,
A symphony of laughter strong.
In every petal, every hue,
A celebration, brave and true.

Whispers of the Woodland

In the woods where squirrels play,
Each rustle is a giggle's way.
Beneath the trees, the secrets flow,
As mushrooms dance in moonlight's glow.

A hedgehog winks, quite out of turn,
While fireflies wink, their lamps all burn.
The wise old owl, with feathers grand,
Looks down and mutters, 'A fine night planned!'

The bunnies hop in pitter-pats,
They'd steal a laugh from snoozy cats.
The branches shake, a chuckle sings,
While nature spins its silly things.

So if you wander through this scene,
Expect the unexpected green.
For laughter hides in every nook,
Just listen close, you'll find a crook.

The Dance of Petals

In gardens bright with colors bold,
The flowers wear the sun like gold.
The tulips twirl and roses sway,
While daisies giggle, 'Come on, play!'

A sunflower bows, a daisy spins,
Each petal shows off with silly grins.
The marigolds clap, make quite a fuss,
As bees hum tunes, creating a bus!

The wind joins in, a partner spry,
It sways the branches, oh so high.
Laughter echoes, all around,
In this floral maze, joy's abound.

So take a step, and join the spree,
In every bloom, there's glee, you'll see.
The dance of petals, light and free,
A vibrant world, with joy, to be!

Sonnet of the Silent Garden

In gardens where the shadows play,
A gnome peeks out, he's here to stay.
With silent steps, he guards the plot,
He chuckles at what he's forgot!

The cabbage rolls a grassy eye,
And whispers, 'Look! A butterfly!'
The roses blush, a shade of red,
While ivy giggles, 'Don't lose your head!'

A sleepy snail, with all its might,
Moves slowly past the pale moonlight.
In every corner, laughter's found,
In this serene, yet silly ground.

Though quiet reigns, the jesters stir,
In every weed, a hidden purr.
So wander forth, and lift your heart,
In this silent place, let joy impart.

The Secret Life of Leaves

Leaves whisper secrets in the breeze,
They gossip loud amongst the trees.
A maple claims it's the best style,
While oaks just laugh and nod awhile.

The birch stands tall, a model proud,
Swaying gently in its crowd.
But in the stillness, watch them sway,
As they tell tales of a bright ballet!

When rain drops fall, they splash around,
Creating puddles on the ground.
In every droplet, they find a song,
A tune that carries all day long.

So if you sit beneath their shade,
Listen close to the tricks they've made.
For every leaf has a story to weave,
In this playful realm, you won't believe!

Stanzas in the Shade

Underneath the leafy crown,
Lizards dance, upside down.
A squirrel wears a tiny hat,
Complaining 'bout his chubby cat.

Flowers gossip, stems all sway,
'Did you hear what Daffodil said today?'
Bumblebees with buzzing cheer,
Are plotting joy or maybe beer.

Sunbeams peek from high above,
To tickle petals, push and shove.
With jokes they twist and turn the day,
In nature's laughter, come what may.

So join the fun, let worries flee,
For even trees crack jokes with glee!
In shade, we find the brightest truth,
Nature's humor, evergreen youth.

The Elegy of Eclipsed Gardens

In gardens dim, where shadows creep,
Flora sighs, it's time for sleep.
A gnome fell down, forgot his pose,
And carrots giggle in their rows.

The daisies mourn a lost bouquet,
While cacti poke with sharp dismay.
A willow whimpers, 'oh, my leaves!'
As ivy wraps around, he grieves.

But wait! The moon begins to play,
With shadows in a grand ballet.
The roses blush, "It's just a phase!"
While pumpkins plot their merry ways.

So cheers to all, in dusk's embrace,
For every frown has its own grace.
In gardens wild, with joy on hand,
We dance beneath the moonlit band.

Refrains of the Rooted

The roots below begin to sing,
They tickle trees, a funny thing!
A beetle struts, a tiny star,
While flowers joke, 'We've come so far!'

"Knock, knock!" buzz a bumble bee,
"Who's there?" "A bloom! Just wait and see!"
With petals bright and faces wide,
They giggle at the world outside.

In twisted vines, old tales unwind,
Of squirrels plotting, schemes aligned.
The thorns all cheer, a prickly shout,
"Grass is greener, no doubt about!"

As sunlight strikes the leafy stage,
Nature's jesters take the page.
In joyful roots, we find our tune,
And laugh along beneath the moon.

The Voice of Verdure

In vibrant hues, the greens collide,
With minty beats and thyme beside.
A chatter from the petaled crew,
"Have you heard what the stalks can do?"

The daisies tease, "We're in full bloom!"
While succulents sing in a sunlight room.
A dandy lion, not shy at all,
Says, "I'm the king of this leafy hall!"

Butterflies flutter, giggles in wind,
Whispers of magic that never rescind.
"Oh, mischief blooms where sunlight beams,
Let's paint the world with laugh and dreams!"

So here's to green, in all its glory,
A green parade, a funny story.
With verdant voices, our hearts entwine,
In nature's laughter, we sip the wine.

Stanzas of Sunlit Serenity

In the garden, bees do dance,
Sun in bloom, they take a chance.
Petals swirl, like giggling girls,
Chasing dreams and summer twirls.

Butterflies wear funny hats,
Flipping 'round like acrobats.
Laughter blooms in every shade,
Nature's joy, a grand parade!

Crickets chirp a merry tune,
Underneath a smiling moon.
They twirl in grass, oh what a sight,
A frolicsome, starry night.

With dandelions in repose,
Tickling toes of all who pose.
Join the fun, don't be shy,
In this laughter, we all fly!

Ballad of the Blossoming Boughs

The branches sway with merry glee,
A jig is led by bumblebee.
A squirrel spins a wild tale,
While flowers spill their sweet detail.

Cherries roll like little jokes,
On laughing limbs, the fun evokes.
"Oh not my hat!" the gardener cries,
As petals flutter 'neath the skies.

The raccoons wear their masks with pride,
As through the leaves they slip and slide.
Each bloom a burst of cheerful jest,
In these woods, we feel our best!

So raise a toast with leafy cheers,
To nature's playful, funny gears.
In this green space, joy is found,
Where every laugh is root-bound!

Nectar of Nostalgia

Oh the scent of elder blooms,
Brings back tales of silly grooms.
A hive of humor, buzzing loud,
In the shade, we share with crowd.

Memories drip like honey sweet,
Sticky fingers, tasty treat.
We gather round the ancient tree,
Laughing 'bout days wild and free.

The petals whisper secrets dear,
In every breeze, a grin, a cheer.
With each drop, a giggle flows,
History's fruit, it brightly glows.

So sip the nectar, let it beam,
Our funny hearts, a bubbling stream.
In every wisp of fragrant air,
Lies laughter's essence everywhere.

Portraits in Petal and Thorn

A rose grins wide, that cheeky bloom,
It's dressed in shades of bold costume.
While daisies roll their eyes with sass,
At prickly friends who dare to pass.

Thorns poke gently, jesting so,
"Watch your step, while we steal the show!"
Each blossom's tale, a comical twist,
In gardens where no punch is missed.

Sunflowers strut, show off their height,
While beetles dance in pure delight.
Pollens float like sparkling confetti,
In this theatre, so bright and petty.

As nightfall wraps its cozy cloak,
The flowers whisper, sharing jokes.
In every petal, every thorn,
Laughter blooms where joy is born!

The Ballad of the Cacti's Embrace

In a desert dance, the cacti sway,
With prickly hugs in sunshine's ray.
They boast of blooms, though few and shy,
A needle jibe—oh me, oh my!

Beneath the moon, their shadows prance,
In pointy shoes, they start to dance.
With every jig, a spine may poke,
Yet laughter fills the starlit smoke.

Their friends, the lizards, join the jest,
In a spiky suit, they feel their best.
A toadstool clown jumps on the floor,
"Cacti, please, just hug no more!"

So here's to spines and laughter shared,
In desert nights, no heart left scared.
With every jibe and sharp retort,
The cacti love, but don't support!

The Harmony of Hidden Hedges

In tangled greens, the hedges hide,
A secret band, all dignified.
With leaves of laughter, twigs of cheer,
They plan a gig that draws them near.

The bunnies hop, wearing disguise,
With floppy ears and twinkly eyes.
As hedges hum, the birds take flight,
A raucous tune in fading light.

A hedgehog strums a leafy lute,
His bristles bounce to each sharp toot.
With every note, a chorus loud,
The thicket sways in weeds so proud.

Yet when the sun begins to set,
The woodland's prank—oh what a bet!
The hedges bend and giggle soft,
In nighttime's hush, they lift aloft!

Rhymes of the Resilient Roots

Down in the dirt, where critters roam,
Roots tell tales of life at home.
They twist and turn in secret glee,
In zany antics, they dance carefree.

With worms as friends, they plot and weave,
Creating laughs that never leave.
"For every storm that shakes our ground,
We'll grow a joke to spread around!"

A beetle joins with rhythmic clap,
As roots yodel and take a nap.
With nutty puns and charming quirks,
They cheer each other's little perks.

So next time you walk through the park,
Remember those roots that leave their mark.
With laughter hidden in each line,
Resilient roots, a friendship fine!

The Muse of Mossy Meadows

In meadows lush, the moss does sit,
A cozy throne, where critters flit.
With hues of green, they weave their lore,
Each tuft a tale behind the door.

The bumblebees with jolly hums,
Join the party where laughter thrums.
A dance of spores, a jig of glee,
They toast to fungi—"Come join us, please!"

With dappled sun and twinkling dew,
The mossy muse brings friends anew.
They twirl about in blushing bloom,
Filling the meadow with sweet perfume.

Now gather round, you sprightly crew,
In meadows bright, there's always room.
With every giggle, let's embrace,
For in this green, we find our place!

The Secret Lives of Stems

In the garden's quiet maze,
Stems gossip through the days.
They twist and sway with grace,
Bragging who's won the race.

With whispers soft as dew,
They challenge flowers too.
"You think you're all that bright?"
"Well, we hold you up so tight!"

A rivalry of height and flair,
With blooms declaring their share.
Yet stems just shake and laugh,
In this leafy aftermath.

Underneath the sun's nice glow,
They crown their wooden show.
For in the end, here's the cheer,
It's all about holding dear.

Verses from the Verdant Vines

Vines giggle as they climb,
Surveying all in prime.
"We twist and turn with fine style,"
"Outshining others by a mile!"

They dangle grapes with flair,
"Who can resist our juicy care?"
With tendrils that play and tease,
They dance in the playful breeze.

Looking down, they mock the grass,
"You'll never reach our class!"
But know this secret truth,
Without roots, we'd be uncouth!

In sun-kissed laughter they thrive,
Making every heart come alive.
For in this merry, green ballet,
Joy's just a vine away!

The Ballad of Blooming Seasons

Spring sings with blooms so bright,
They whisper secrets, pure delight.
Petals preen in morning light,
"Look at us! We're quite the sight!"

Summer dances in bold hues,
Flowers flaunt their vibrant views.
"Catch my color, can you see?"
"In this garden, I'm the key!"

Autumn's hues offer jest,
As leaves fall, they take their rest.
"It's a colorful cascade!"
"Let's party before we fade!"

Winter winks and wraps them tight,
Buds dream of spring's return bright.
So every season finds its place,
In nature's timeless, funny race.

A Tapestry of Thorns

Thorns chuckle in prickly might,
As roses bask in pure delight.
"We're the guards of this fine crew,"
"Hey, don't prick us—just pass through!"

With sharp wit and humor keen,
They keep the garden serene.
"You'll need a armor to stroll!"
"Or in our realm, you won't be whole!"

Yet roses bloom with charm that sways,
"Together we'll conquer every phase!"
Though thorns have their pointy game,
They laugh as all cast a name.

In nature's oddity, they cleave,
Making peace, though hard to believe.
For even thorns know with some fun,
A garden thrives when joy is spun.

A Dance with Dandelions

Dandelions dance in the breeze,
Spinning round with utmost ease.
They blow their seeds like tiny kites,
Waving goodbye with all their might.

In a grassy field, they twirl and prance,
Inviting bees to join their dance.
Each flower laughs, a golden face,
Chasing bugs in a wild chase.

A gathering of bright yellow cheer,
With every gust, they disappear.
But don't you fret, they'll reappear,
In every crack, they're always near.

So if you see a dandy wild,
Just watch it twirl, a carefree child.
And maybe join this flower craze,
For life is short; let's dance and gaze!

Lullaby of the Lush Landscape

In a meadow bright and wide,
Grass and flowers take a ride.
Bumblebees hum their sleepy tune,
While daisies nod beneath the moon.

Butterflies waltz on gentle air,
As crickets croon without a care.
The willow weeps, but smiles inside,
Swaying softly, a leafy guide.

Amidst the leaves, a squirrel peeks,
Chasing dreams for a thousand weeks.
He stashes nuts like hidden gold,
In this landscape, stories unfold.

As stars blanket this sleepy scene,
Nature giggles in shades of green.
The lullaby whispers low and sweet,
In dreams of nature, we find our beat.

The Silent Serenade of Saplings

Little saplings stand so tall,
Whisper secrets, tiny call.
Roots entwined beneath the ground,
A silent song in shades profound.

They stretch their limbs with sleepy grace,
A giggle hides in their embrace.
Leaves quiver in the morning light,
Poking fun at birds in flight.

With every breeze, they sway and bend,
Sharing tales, as branches blend.
Each gust a jest, a playful tease,
In this shady grove, they find their ease.

So next time you pass by so keen,
Remember the whispers unseen.
For in the wood, beneath the sun,
Saplings chuckle, life's a pun!

Chronicles of the Canopy

In the canopy high above,
All the creatures dance and shove.
Squirrels leap like acrobats,
While monkeys giggle, wearing hats.

Leaves like curtains, shades of green,
Hide stories rich and rarely seen.
The owl hoots with wisdom old,
Of tales that nightly trees have told.

A parrot squawks with vivid flair,
Chasing clouds through perfumed air.
Each branch a stage for nature's play,
Where trees prance on a sunny day.

So listen well when next you roam,
The canopy holds a vibrant home.
For every rustle and every cheer,
In green, there's magic, always near.

Twilight Whispers of the Tulips

In the garden where tulips play,
They sway and twirl at the end of day.
A bug hums tunes that make them blush,
While bumblebees join in the rush.

Oh listen close, the flowers giggle,
Tickling petals make the wind wiggle.
The sun slips low, the shadows creep,
As tulips whisper secrets, not for sleep.

With their bright hats, they dance so free,
Sipping raindrops like cups of tea.
They shout, "We're the best, just take a look!"
While fairies sit reading their flower book.

So when twilight slips into the night,
Remember the tulips and their delight.
For in their laughter, joy blooms wide,
And every leaf holds a giggling pride.

The Poetry of Prickly Pears

Amongst the cacti, prickly pears stand,
With sharp little hats that demand attention grand.
They chuckle together, all spiky and sweet,
In a prickly club where the green fruit meet.

"Don't touch us here, we'll give you a jab!"
They warn with a grin, a spiky little fab.
While sipping the sun, they prattle and jest,
Flirting with flowers, feeling quite blessed.

They throw a party, the desert's alive,
With saguaro siblings, they leap and thrive.
Underneath stars, they dance without care,
While the moon casts a glow on their prickly affair.

So if you find them, just stop and stare,
These humorous fruits have stories to share.
For in their poise, there's a playful cheer,
That tickles the cactus and softens the fear.

Anthem of the Acorns

Acorns gather on the old oak tree,
With tiny hats, they giggle with glee.
"Let's roll down the hill, a chipmunk parade!
We'll charm all the squirrels, our friends are unmade!"

They tumble and bounce, then start to conspire,
In whispered tones, they share their desire.
A life full of mischief, a nutty delight,
With laughter and joy, they dance through the night.

"Oh, watch that branch! It's bending with cheer,
We'll swing from the leaves, let go of our fear!"
They clap and they shout, with each little plop,
While fellas below say, "Don't let it stop!"

In autumn's soft glow, they wear colors bold,
These cheeky acorns, a sight to behold.
With dreams of the winter, and all that can be,
Their anthem of joy rings through every tree.

Harmonies of the Herbaceous

In the soil where herbs have a laugh,
Oregano winks, and thyme splits a chaff.
"Let's sing with the parsley, our green little friend,
We'll dance in the garden till daylight's end!"

Basil bursts out in a fragrant delight,
Joining the chorus, the herbs feel so bright.
With garlic and chives, they hum a sweet tune,
While butterflies sway underneath the moon.

"Who needs a chef when we have our flair?
Let's spice up the dinner, make everyone stare!"
They giggle and sway in the warm summer air,
With laughter that perfumes the world everywhere.

So when you stroll through the gardens so green,
Remember the chorus of herbs and their sheen.
For in their vibrations, joy sings like a bell,
These merry green wonders infuse life so well.

Tales from the Thicket

In a thicket dense and green,
A squirrel danced, a funny scene.
He twirled and spun with nut in hand,
Declaring victory o'er the land.

The hedgehog joined, in spiky coat,
Said, "I can beat you, just watch me float!"
With bated breath, they both took flight,
But landed squished; oh, what a sight!

The rabbit chuckled, sipping dew,
"Next time, fellas, bring a crew!"
But all agreed, with laughter grand,
Their antics made the best of plans.

So in the thicket, tales unfold,
Of dancing nuts and brave and bold.
The forest echoes with their cheer,
Where laughter blooms, the best this year!

An Epic of Evergreen Echoes

Through evergreen halls, the pine trees sway,
As a raccoon plots his buffet day.
He snacks on berries, oh what a feast!
He's more than a bandit; he's quite the beast!

The deer looked on with wide-eyed glee,
"Do save some greens for you and me!"
But the raccoon grinned, with a wink and a laugh,
"Join me instead, let's split the path!"

The ferns held hands, a leafy brigade,
As they laughed at the pranks that nature made.
"Let's play a game, who can stand still?
The bird on the branch has all the skill!"

Thus echoes of joy rang through the trees,
In a forest filled with sillies and tease.
And folklore grew in the light of day,
Of frolicking critters, in their funny way!

The Script of Sunflowers

In a field where sunflowers stand so tall,
They gossip and giggle, as petals enthrall.
"One day we'll dance in the soft summer rain,
But first, let's complain about the way we're vain!"

A bumblebee buzzed, with a cheeky remark,
"Looking too fine, may cause quite the spark!"
"Shoo!" yelled one flower, flailing with glee,
"Keep your stinger away, or you'll taste my tea!"

As evening fell, they dipped and swayed,
The moonlight shining, and mischief played.
"Watch me twist!" one sunflower cried,
"Oh dear, get a grip!"—the others replied.

In this sunny patch, a party unfolds,
With whispers and laughter, and tales retold.
For the script of the flowers, so silly and bright,
Is a comedy show, under the starry night!

The Diary of Dew-kissed Petals

Dew kissed softly on petals' grace,
In a diary kept where blooms embrace.
Each day a story, fresh to tell,
Of bees in hugs and the wind's sweet swell.

"Oh what a neighbor!" the rosebud sighed,
"Bloom's so thick that he can't bide!"
But tulips chimed with a vibrant jest,
"Let's paint the world and be our best!"

In the morning light, the blossoms sway,
Sharing their secrets in a funny way.
"I'll wear my colors, bold and loud,
For a splash of joy—let's make it proud!"

So flip through the leaves of petals' tales,
With laughter blooming as joy prevails.
In this garden where giggles reign,
The funny diary will never wane!

Echoes in the Evergreen

In the forest, trees hold chats,
Squirrels play their silly prats.
Branches bow to gossip now,
Waves of green, take a bow.

Mice in suits, with little ties,
Dance beneath the laughing skies.
Oak and pine, they spin and twirl,
While daisies start to giggle and whirl.

Rabbits wearing floppy hats,
Join the chorus, squeaks and claps.
Nature's stage, a jolly sight,
Every leaf, a laugh, so bright.

When sunbeams peek and shadows race,
The forest holds its wild embrace.
In echoes sweet, the trees enthrall,
With laughter shared, they have a ball.

The Language of Leaves

Whispers float on breezy tales,
Leaves exchange their funny gales.
Maples giggle, willows sigh,
While alders wink, oh my, oh my!

Petals laugh in gentle sways,
As blossoms join with jolly plays.
They conspire to tickle the air,
Nature's jests everywhere!

Bumblebees buzz in playful hums,
Pollinating all the fun crumbs.
A sunflower cracks a golden smile,
Turning heads, it spans a mile.

Sprightly vines entwine in glee,
Nature's jesters, wild and free.
A dance of green, a joyful tease,
In every rustle, a joyful breeze.

Ode to the Orchid's Grace

Orchids wear a crown of flair,
Strutting their stuff with utmost care.
In colors bright, they floss and boast,
While bumblebees play proud host.

Swaying like they're on a stage,
Each petal holds its own true sage.
With cheeky smiles, they shout, 'Hooray!'
In gardens where the mischief plays.

Laughter rings through every bloom,
As jasmine scents the prescient room.
The daisies cheer, the poppies chuckle,
In this floral giggle, there's no struggle.

With roots that dance and stems that prance,
Orchids teach us how to dance.
So join the fun, let worries cease,
In nature's mirth, we find our peace.

Garden of Gossamer Dreams

In a garden where fairies dwell,
Every flower has a tale to tell.
Butterflies flit in silly races,
Tickling petals, playing with faces.

Here, the dahlias wear bright hats,
Chitchatting with ruffled chats.
Snapdragons grin, their jaws agape,
Wishing for a friend escape.

Gentle breezes carry jest,
A whimsical place, a magical nest.
In glimmers soft, the dreams unfurl,
As nature laughs, we all twirl.

So come and dance on soft green beds,
Join in the fun where laughter spreads.
In this garden, open your seams,
And frolic through gossamer dreams.

Chants of the Cherry Blossoms

In springtime's glee they dance and sway,
The cherry trees have much to say.
With giggles sweet, their petals fall,
A pink parade, oh such a ball!

Bees are buzzing, quite the show,
Confused by scents they do not know.
They bump and fumble, round they go,
A sticky mess, how funny though!

Kids beneath the branches leap,
As petals rain like dreams in sleep.
They swipe and catch with open hands,
As laughter spills across the lands!

So let us sing of blooms that tease,
And party hard in blooming breeze.
With cherry cheeks and joyful calls,
We celebrate the cherry balls!

Symphony of the Swaying Stems

The stems they sway in sunny cheer,
A leafy dance, oh so sincere.
With every breeze, a rustle sounds,
As laughter fills the vibrant grounds.

The daisies giggle, shirts of white,
While hipster blooms wear shades so bright.
They pose and preen, quite unaware,
That nature laughs without a care.

A dandelion's puff goes poof,
In windy jokes, it loses proof.
It scatters seeds like silly dreams,
Each floating by, or so it seems!

So sway along, ye swaying stems,
Join in the fun of floral hymns.
Together let our voices raise,
In nature's quirky, leafy praise!

Tales from the Thicket

In thickets deep where shadows play,
The critters dance by break of day.
With twigs for hats and leaves for dress,
They host a party, what a mess!

The rabbits hop, the squirrels spin,
A whiskered grin on every chin.
While hedgehogs roll in gentle glee,
They join the fun with jubilee!

The flowers join, they shake their stems,
While butterflies become the gems.
In laughter shared, the thicket sings,
Of joyful hearts and silly things!

So gather round, oh friends so dear,
In thickets wild, let's shed a tear.
Of laughter bright and tales in tow,
In nature's glee, the joy will grow!

The Garden's Gentle Lullaby

In gardens grand where flowers dream,
A gentle song begins to stream.
With buzzing bees and rustling leaves,
The garden hums, oh how it weaves!

The daisies nod, the lilies sway,
They gossip soft throughout the day.
Each petal tells a funny tale,
Of sun-kissed dreams that never fail.

The veggies giggle, roots entwined,
With carrots and peas, how they unwind!
They share their tales of soil and sun,
A cheeky bunch, oh what fun!

So close your eyes and breathe it in,
The garden's song, where laughs begin.
With gentle rhythms, all is well,
In lullabies of bloom, we dwell!

Songs of the Saffron Sunset

The sun wore a saffron gown,
Frolicking right over town.
Chickens danced, the goats did twirl,
In this jolly, golden whirl.

Bees buzzed a tune with delight,
While flowers giggled in the light.
The daisies tried to steal the show,
But all the sunflowers stole the glow.

A caterpillar sang of leaves,
While the ants laughed at their thieves.
Oh, what a party in the field,
Where laughter and sunshine wouldn't yield.

As twilight painted all in red,
Silly shadows danced instead.
The moon rolled in, a chuckling sprite,
Promising more fun by night.

The Fable of Ferns

A fern decided it could fly,
With tiny wings, it kissed the sky.
But all it did was sway and bend,
Like a ballerina without end.

The spiders made their tiny bets,
On which could weave the silliest nets.
The butterfly queens skipped with glee,
While winking at the dancing bee.

A wise old tree with roots so deep,
Said laughter's something you can't keep.
The ferns just giggled, green and spry,
And claimed they'd fly by simply trying high.

So if you see a fern take flight,
It's just a trick of playful light.
Join the fun and laugh a while,
Nature's a stage, so wear a smile.

Echoing Euphoria of the Earth

The earth sings in a chuckling tone,
Where mushrooms giggle and seeds are sown.
A rabbit hops with a joyful flair,
Telling flowers secrets it can't share.

The sunflowers trade their sunny looks,
Reading gossip in the nature books.
While crickets play their chirpy games,
And ants come marching, calling names.

A bush chatted wildly to the breeze,
Whispering tales of mischief with ease.
The rocks rolled in, quite full of cheer,
Saying, "We belong, let's dance right here!"

So listen close, and you might hear,
The funny stories of the year.
With nature's glee all around your feet,
You'll find all things composting sweet.

Verses from the Verdant

In the verdant grove, a squirrel pranced,
Wearing a hat, he boldly danced.
The daisies chuckled in their beds,
As the robin teased with its bright red threads.

Laughter erupted from the tall grass,
Where grasshoppers leapt—quite the class!
They wore tiny ties, a splendid sight,
Debating the best ways to take flight.

A flower said, "I bloom quite well,"
But the cactus piped, "I've tales to tell!"
With prickly humor and lots of cheer,
They shared their jokes, loud and clear.

So next time you roam the green embrace,
Join the laughter in every space.
For in every leaf and every sprout,
Giggles of nature are what it's about.

The Rhythm of Raindrops and Roots

Raindrops dance on thirsty leaves,
The squirrels slide in muddy cleaves.
Flowers giggle in bright parade,
While worms do the cha-cha in the shade.

Bees buzz tunes of sweet surprise,
As daisies wink with sunny eyes.
The grasshoppers hop, in perfect sync,
While frogs croak choruses - what a link!

Mud pies are served at the garden feast,
And ants hold a party, to say the least.
As thunder claps, they twirl about,
In nature's laughter, there's no doubt.

So when the rain drops from above,
It's not just water, it's a dance of love.
Join the fun, let your spirit soar,
In fields of giggles; there's always more.

Melodic Treasures of the Tangle

In tangled vines, a concert's found,
With ukulele frogs making sound.
The leaves rustle in cheer and glee,
While crickets play their symphony.

Sunflowers sway to the breezy beat,
While beetles shuffle to their feet.
A raccoon joins with a trumpet spin,
As blooms jog along with a playful grin.

Thistles twirl in a disco trance,
While butterflies flutter, joining the dance.
Mushrooms gather for a midnight show,
Under the moon's soft, silver glow.

In this jungle of fun and cheer,
Every creature holds music dear.
So grab a partner, let's take a whirl,
In nature's gallery, watch life unfurl.

Petal Poesy

Petals whisper secrets sweet,
As butterflies flitter, oh so neat.
A daffodil winks, oh so sly,
While roses giggle as bees pass by.

Tulips tap dance in sunny spots,
While violets strum on flower pots.
Pansies laugh, their eyes so bright,
While daisies plan a garden flight.

In every corner, a joke takes root,
With ladybugs wearing tiny boots.
Laughter blooms where friendships grow,
In every petal, joy does flow.

So let's compose this floral rhyme,
Each flower adds its splendid chime.
With petals soft and spirits light,
We find our joy from day till night.

The Timeless Bloom

In gardens old where laughter reigns,
Each petal spins with playful chains.
The daisies nod, the lilies sway,
As nature's jesters join the play.

Silly stems in a comical rush,
Chasing shadows in a sunny hush.
Cacti chuckle while crows caw loud,
In the orchestra of green, we're all proud.

The bumblebees wear tiny hats,
While beetles chat about their spats.
The lilac's note serves as a cue,
For all the blooms to sing anew.

So raise a glass to the blooms so bright,
With laughter echoing into the night.
In the timeless garden, joy abounds,
Where every laugh with nature resounds.

The Chronicle of Climbing Ferns

In a garden of fronds, they dance and sway,
With laughter they climb, in their leafy ballet.
Twisting and turning, they reach for the skies,
Ferns in a frenzy, oh what a surprise!

They whisper of secrets, and giggle with glee,
Sharing wild tales of a vine's jubilee.
A feast of green laughter, they twirl and they spin,
In this realm of the ferns, let the fun begin!

With roots deep in mischief, they play hide and seek,
In the shade of each leaf, you'll find them all week.
The sunbeams will tickle, they flourish, they tease,
Oh, what a time with the climbing green breeze!

So join in the party, no need for a crown,
In the realm of the ferns, we can all wear a gown.
With laughter and joy, let the feasting commence,
In this leafy lore, we find such immense!

Bards of the Botanical Haven

Gathered beneath trees, with a twinkle of cheer,
The bards of the garden sing songs loud and clear.
With petals for paper, and sap for their ink,
They weave tales of roses, and daisies that blink.

Each note is a petal, each word sprinkles light,
In harmony blending, they shine oh so bright.
A symphony sacred, of critters and blooms,
As crickets keep time, the laughter resumes.

From tulips to sunflowers, each chorus a gift,
The chorus of chlorophyll offers a lift.
With humor in verses, and puns in the leaves,
The bards of the haven spin joy like a breeze.

So come, join their revel, strum chords made of vines,
In the laughter of flora, share drinks made of twines.
With each little giggle, let spirits take flight,
In this botanical haven, all's merry and bright!

Rhapsody of Rustling Foliage

In the rustling leaves, where the whispers reside,
The rustle and tussle, nature's wild ride.
Each shiver and quiver, a giggle, a grin,
In the foliage's dance, let the mischief begin!

The shrubs throw a party, the branches all sway,
Inviting the breezes to come out and play.
A rhapsody sings, with a tickle and tease,
As the foliage frolics, all share in the breeze.

With squirrels assisting in antics so grand,
Chasing each other, each leaf in a hand.
They'll leap and they'll bound, in a playful parade,
In the rhapsody merry, bright colors cascade.

So dance with the leaves, let the laughter ensue,
For in whispers and rustles, we find something new.
A symphony of joy, where nature's alive,
In the rhapsody playful, we all will thrive!

Celebrations of the Citrus Grove

In the grove of bright citrons, the laughter resounds,
With oranges grinning in round, juicy crowns.
Lemon trees frolic with zesty delight,
As tangy confetti bursts forth with each bite.

The grapefruits are dancing, each twirl full of cheer,
As limes join the fun, with a wink and a sneer.
A fiesta of flavors, oh what a scene,
With fruit-juiced giggles, and zest that's so keen!

From cocktails to picnics, the joy never fades,
In the shade of the branches, a party cascades.
Citrus juicers cheer, with all of their might,
In this grove of delight, there's never a night.

So raise up your glasses, let fruity fun flow,
In the bright, sunny grove, where the laughter will grow.
With a swirl and a sip, let the festivities thrive,
In the citrusy laughter, we all feel alive!

Aria of the Ancient Arbor

Under the oak, the squirrels dance,
In acorn hats, they take their chance.
Beneath a bough, a rabbit sings,
While bees hum tunes of buzzing flings.

A crow cracks jokes from lofty heights,
Joking with leaves in daylight sights.
The trees all chuckle at his puns,
As shadows play and laughter runs.

A fox in shades, so sleek and sly,
Winks at the flowers, waving hi.
Grasshoppers join in for a show,
With leaps and bounds, they steal the glow.

Old branches sway, they twist and bend,
Creating shuffles, they do not end.
The air turns light with whimsy's breath,
In this old grove, there's life and jest.

Chronicles of the Chrysanthemum

In the garden, blooms so bright,
Chrysanthemums put on a fight.
They boast their colors, crisp and grand,
With petals fanning, they take a stand.

A bumblebee, in a tuxedo fine,
Bumbles around, misjudging the vine.
His dance is clumsy, yet it's a show,
As he trips on petals, then tips in the flow.

The daisies giggle, rolling their eyes,
As tulips plot their colorful lies.
'Who wore it best?' they slyly claim,
While buttercups join in on the game.

At dusk, the crickets chirp in tune,
Adding to tales beneath the moon.
In this kingdom, laughter reigns,
Amongst the blooms, joy never wanes.

Whispers of the Wildflowers

Wildflowers chat in hues so bright,
Swapping secrets under the light.
The daisies gossip, the violets tease,
While poppies sway in the soft summer breeze.

A caterpillar, dressed in green,
Wiggles by, a sight to be seen.
He's plotting tricks on the nearby ants,
Who march along in disciplined chants.

Butterflies float with dazzling grace,
Laughing at beetles in a silly race.
With each flutter, they spread the cheer,
In the wild, there's nothing to fear.

As twilight drops its silken veil,
The wildflowers share their nightly tale.
In laughter, they twinkle, sparkle, and glow,
Together in nature's grand show.

Serene Symphony of Saplings

Little saplings sway with glee,
In their tiny roots, they find the key.
Bouncing gently in the morning sun,
Singing softly, they say, 'Let's run!'

A curious worm peeks from below,
He wiggles high, putting on a show.
"Join me, friends, let's start a band!"
And all the buds lend a leafy hand.

Sunshine tickles their tender leaves,
As they dance along, no room for thieves.
The wind blows strong, with a hearty laugh,
Turning their giggles into a chaff.

With every breeze, a tune they form,
In nature's house, there's always warmth.
Saplings smile and sway in style,
Creating joys that last a while.

www.ingramcontent.com/pod-product-compliance
Lightning Source LLC
Chambersburg PA
CBHW070748220426
43209CB00083B/118